AMERICAN
DEMOCRACY
IN ACTION

Laws and the Judicial System

Cathleen Small

LUCENT
PRESS

Published in 2019 by
Lucent Press, an Imprint of Greenhaven Publishing, LLC
353 3rd Avenue
Suite 255
New York, NY 10010

Produced for Lucent by Calcium Creative Ltd
Designers: Clare Webber and Simon Borrough
Picture researcher: Rachel Blount
Editors: Sarah Eason and Jennifer Sanderson

Picture credits: Cover: Victoria Lipov (top), Sirtravelalot (bottom). Inside: Shutterstock: Africa
Studio: p. 12; ArtOlympic: p. 10; BortN66: p. 9; Boyphare: p. 21; Dado Photos: p. 20; Drop
of Light: p. 17; Everett Historical: pp. 30, 37, 42; Hogan Imaging: p. 43; Hquality: p. 34; Ilya
Images: p. 7; Glynnis Jones: p. 14; RenysView: p. 25; Tinnaporn Sathapornnanont: p. 6; Rena
Schild: p. 39; Joe Seer: p. 26; Sopotnicki: p. 23; Tommaso79: p. 33; Tupungato: p. 24; Rex
Wholster: p. 27; Zimmytws: pp. 5, 13, 19, 44-45; Zolnierek: p. 8; Chad Zuber: p. 29; Wikimedia
Commons: U.S. Air National Guard photo by Staff Sgt. Lealan Buehrer: p. 16; John Stephen
Dwyer: p. 41.

Cataloging-in-Publication Data

Names: Small, Cathleen.
Title: Laws and the judicial system / Cathleen Small.
Description: New York : Lucent Press, 2019. | Series: American democracy in action |
Includes glossary and index.
Identifiers: ISBN 9781534564053 (pbk.) | ISBN 9781534564039 (library bound)
Subjects: LCSH: Courts--United States--Juvenile literature. | Law--United States--
Interpretation and construction--Juvenile literature. | Justice, Administration of--United
States--Juvenile literature.
Classification: LCC KF8720.S63 2019 | DDC 347.73'2--dc23

Printed in the United States of America

CPSIA compliance information: Batch #BS18KL: For further information, contact
Greenhaven Publishing, LLC, New York, New York, at 1-844-317-7404.

Please visit our website, www.greenhavenpublishing.com. For a free color catalog of all our
high-quality books, call toll free 1-844-317-7404 or fax 1-844-317-7405.

Contents

CHAPTER 1

The U.S. Judicial System

When the **Framers of the Constitution** were setting forth the ideals and goals under which the United States would function, they felt that a separation of powers was necessary. That is, the new country could not risk one person or a small group of people taking too much power and control over the nation. They decided that the best way to avoid this was to structure the government so that the power was divided among multiple branches of government. This is how the United States came to be governed by three main branches of power: the executive branch, the legislative branch, and the judicial branch.

The Executive Branch of Government

The executive branch consists of the president and vice president, and a number of people and agencies that work directly under them. The executive branch has many functions, but one is ensuring the common good of the nation. This includes supporting legislation, or laws, that will best serve all U.S. citizens.

The Legislative Branch of Government

The legislative branch is made up of the two chambers of Congress: the Senate and the House of Representatives. It is this branch that is mainly responsible for passing and amending laws. The president can suggest new laws, but they alone cannot pass them. Laws begin as bills, which must be formally proposed by a member of Congress.

The United States Constitution specifies that the government's power be divided among three branches: the executive, the legislative, and the judicial. This ensures that no one branch has more power than the others.

Bills go through a long and detailed process of reading, analyzing, and revising before they are finally voted on and moved to the next chamber of Congress. Only new legislation that has been voted in favor of in both chambers of Congress moves on to the president to be officially signed into law.

The Judicial Branch of Government

The third branch of government is the judicial branch. This is the branch responsible for upholding the laws that are in the Constitution and those passed by the legislative branch. If a citizen or group violates federal law, they are tried through the courts that make up the judicial branch.

The judicial branch is strongly tied to the legislative branch, since the legislative branch makes the laws that the judicial branch upholds. However, the judicial branch is not entirely separate from the executive branch, either. The president is responsible for appointing justices to the Supreme Court, which is the highest court in the U.S. court system. He also appoints justices to the circuit courts, which are one step below the Supreme Court, and the district courts, which are just below the circuit courts. The president's nomination has to be confirmed by the Senate, so the legislative branch is also involved in this process.

In this way, there is a system of checks and balances that ensures that no one branch of government has too much power. This keeps the United States from becoming a **dictatorship** or an **oligarchy**.

State Judicial Systems

As a whole, the United States has a judicial system designed to uphold the Constitution and the federal laws that have been put in place since its signing. However, because states in the U.S. are **sovereign**, they also each have their own judicial systems.

The Supreme Court is the highest court in the United States. Like many important government buildings, it is located in Washington, D.C.

Before reaching the Supreme Court, most cases are tried in lower courts. They are tried either at the state or federal level, depending on the case.

When a person or group violates a state or local law, they are tried through the judicial system in their own state. Depending on the violation, they may be tried through the federal judicial system, but often their trial and punishment are handled at the state level.

If a party does not accept legal judgment handed to it at the state level, there may be instances when the case is taken to the federal courts. In some cases, the legal violation in question violates state and federal laws, so it could technically be tried in either court. In other cases, a party may have exhausted all state-level appeals and may attempt to take the case higher, such as to the Supreme Court. This is not a very common occurrence, but it has happened in cases in which the rulings have a significant effect on the U.S. public as a whole. For example, there have been **civil rights** cases in which the parties have started a suit at the state level and eventually taken it all the way to the Supreme Court—largely because the ruling affects not just them, but the entire population.

All of the state and federal courts, the law-enforcement professionals who protect the public and apprehend law violaters, and the lawyers who plead their clients' cases, work together to uphold the laws of the United States and ensure public safety.

CHAPTER 2

Making Laws

Not all laws are created equally. Laws are made and enforced at different levels of government, and some take precedence over others. In general, the U.S. Constitution is considered the supreme law of the land, and constitutional law takes precedence over laws made at lower levels of the government. However, not all cases are ruled on by constitutional law. Generally, if a crime is committed, it is a violation of a law at a lower level, and it is punished as such.

Law at the Local Level

Local laws are usually called ordinances. They are formed at a local level, such as by city, county, or **municipality**. There are some rules behind their formation, in an attempt to not duplicate laws that have already been passed at a higher level. This varies a bit by state, but in all states, cities and counties are allowed to create local ordinances for criminal offenses punishable at the state level. They can do this if the punishment according to the local ordinance is greater than the punishment at the state level.

In other words, there are state laws in effect for many crimes. Take murder as an example. For a city or county to pass a local ordinance covering the penalty for murder, the punishment needs to be greater than the punishment at state level.

The gavel and Lady Justice are symbols of the law. The gavel represents authority, and Lady Justice is symbolic of the moral force of the law.

After an arrest, a person can be tried only under one law. Many cases are tried at the state level.

If the state sees murder as an offense punishable by 30 years in prison, the local ordinance would have to set the punishment at greater than 30 years.

Some states also set limitations on what local ordinances can cover. Maryland, for example, does not allow local ordinances to be passed on topics related to firearms possession and gun control.

It is also important to note that when a criminal offense is involved, a person can be charged only under one law for a particular offense. So, for example, if there are state laws and local ordinances covering drunk-driving offenses, a person can be charged with drunk driving. But they can only be charged under either state or local law, not both. This is as a result of the Fifth Amendment to the Constitution, which has a double-jeopardy clause stating that a person cannot be charged twice for the same crime.

HOW WELL DO YOU UNDERSTAND AMERICAN DEMOCRACY?

Some towns have very strange local ordinances. For example, in a particular city in Connecticut, it is illegal for a beautician to hum, whistle, or sing while cutting hair. Do some research to find out what unusual ordinances your town has.

Local ordinances can cover almost anything, as long as they follow the rules for not duplicating state laws. Often, local ordinances cover issues that are important at the local level but would not be particularly important at the state level. For example, the normal speed limit in a residential neighborhood is 25 miles per hour (40 kph). However, a particular **subdivision** might want the speed limit in its community lowered to 10 miles per hour (16 kph), so the subdivision might work to pass a local ordinance to do so.

Exactly how ordinances are passed varies from state to state. However, certain parts of the process are usually the same, regardless of the state. Anyone, from local politicians and councils to committees and private citizens, can propose an idea for a new ordinance. When private citizens have an idea for a local ordinance, they may gather together other citizens with similar interests and present their plan to the appropriate local committee or council, or they may petition to show interest in their idea.

There are approximately 18,000 federal, state, local, and city police departments in the United States. The powers, responsibilities, and funding for police forces vary from state to state. But all police forces must ensure that all laws are upheld.

When enough interest is shown in an ordinance, it is drafted into a proposal that is reviewed by the city council, any related commissions or committees, and any boards that have an interest in it. Generally, the city council will pay attention to committee findings about the pros and cons of the ordinance, and listen to public comment on it. Sometimes a specialized committee will be formed to further investigate the impacts the proposed ordinance might have.

A proposed ordinance generally goes through many cycles of review, comment, and revision before it is finally voted on. Eventually, the city council votes on the proposed ordinance. Sometimes, it must also be approved by the mayor, though that depends on the city or town where the ordinance is proposed. If the ordinance is approved, it will take effect in the specific locality, based on the time and process common there.

Law at the State Level

As each state is set up as sovereign, it has its own state constitution, state government, and state judicial system. States are all still part of the greater United States, which means federal law can take the place of state law where appropriate. However, as a general rule, states are given a lot of flexibility in implementing their own laws and policies.

For example, in recent times, the state of California has been at odds with the Trump administration. The Trump administration does not support climate change science and environmental protections as much as the California government does. So, while the Trump administration rolls back environmental regulations, California continues to act independently and enforce strict environmental regulations.

That sort of process is fine with the federal government as long as California as a state is not violating any federal laws—which it is not. California does not need to declare independence from the United States because of differing views. It simply enacts state-level policies that reflect the values and goals of many of its citizens.

Texas is a good example on the **conservative** side. Abortion laws have been heavily relaxed at a federal level for quite some time. However, Texas is a conservative state with a large number of pro-life supporters. At the state level, Texas tends to discourage flexible abortion laws as much as possible. As with California, Texas is still part of the greater United States. It simply enacts state legislation and policies that reflect the values of many of its residents.

State law governs most of the actions of people in the United States. When a person is charged with a crime, it is most often litigated, or taken to court, at a state level in state courts for claims made under state law. For example, a domestic-violence case would most often be litigated at the state level, not the federal level.

The Supreme Court legalized same-sex marriage in 2015, but the Texas Supreme Court ruled that same-sex couples are not entitled to full marriage benefits in 2017.

Contract law can become difficult when it involves parties in more than one state. In some cases, lawyers and judges look to past rulings to make fair decisions.

State law is sufficient to protect the victim and enact a penalty for the perpetrator, so there is no need to go beyond state law.

Most state law is based on British common law, since much of the United States developed from British colonization and the eventual westward expansion. However, Louisiana state law tends to be more heavily based on French and Spanish law, since it was originally colonized by the French and Spanish.

Regardless of what state law is based on, all state laws have evolved over the years, and no two states have exactly the same laws. This can create some problems when issues cross state lines. For example, if a contract covers services taking place in two states, which state's laws does the contract follow? And how strictly? Some states adhere very strictly to what has been **codified** into law, whereas other states allow judges some freedom in interpreting laws. In the case of a contract, sometimes rulings have to be made based on case law. When there is no specific law covering how to enact a particular contract, lawyers and judges have to look at past contracts to determine what seems fair and unbiased.

So at the state level, the law is fairly clear and well defined, although the extent to which it can be interpreted varies. However, when an issue crosses state lines, things can become more complicated.

Some state laws were created simply by current state laws being codified into legal codes. For example, at the time state legal codes were being created, whatever general processes were currently being followed by the state were recorded and codified into law. However, when new state laws are created, there is a much more complicated process.

New State Laws

Anyone—even a private citizen—can think of a new law. But, a legislator must write the proposal for the new bill and sponsor it. Once that person has done so, the bill is introduced to the chamber of state government in which the sponsor participates. It is read, given a number, and assigned to the appropriate committee for further study.

The committee will then research and discuss the proposed legislation, and it will generally open it up for public comment. The committee will make any needed changes to the bill, based on its research and public comment.

City mayors can propose local laws. In 2015, the First Lady of New York City, Chirlane McCray, announced legislation proposed by her husband Mayor Bill de Blasio.

The committee has several options at that point. It can:

- Pass the bill and send it to the chamber floor for consideration
- Pass the bill and send it on to another committee for further review
- Pass the bill and put it on the consent calendar (this is generally for noncontroversial bills)
- Send the bill to the floor or to another committee without any recommendations
- Vote down the bill
- Table the bill (in theory, for later discussion)
- Ignore the bill
- Return the bill to its sponsor for revision

If the bill passes out of the committee, it will be scheduled for discussion and debate by the entire chamber. At some point, it will be put on the calendar for a vote by all members on the chamber floor.

If the bill passes the vote by all members of the chamber, it then moves on to the other chamber of state government. There, it goes through the same process of committee research, comment, and a floor vote. If the bill passes the second chamber with the same terms as it did in the first chamber, then it is sent to the governor for their signature.

The bill can also pass the second chamber with different terms from the bill that passed the first chamber. In that case, the two chambers must reconcile and produce one bill that is agreed on by both chambers. Sometimes, this happens through one chamber agreeing to the other chamber's version. But often, the bills will go to a conference committee made up of senators and representatives from the two chambers. There, an amended bill that is acceptable to both chambers is hashed out. When that happens, the amended bill is read and voted on in both chambers. If both chambers vote to proceed, the revised bill is sent for the governor's signature.

The governor can sign the bill into law or **veto** it. If the governor vetoes the bill, it can either be a veto of the entire bill or a veto of certain lines in the bill.

UNDERSTANDING VETOES

A full veto of a bill means the governor does not accept any part of the bill. A line-item veto means that the governor accepts some, but not all, of the bill. If the governor takes no action on the bill and the session of the legislature ends, it is known as a pocket veto. The bill is essentially dead, even though the governor did not outright veto it.

However, vetoes are not always the last word. When the governor vetoes a bill, it goes back to the state legislature for reconsideration. If two-thirds of both the state Senate and the House vote to pass the bill, they can overturn the governor's veto and pass the bill into law.

On the left is Bruce Rauner, governor of Illinois. In July 2017, Rauner vetoed a budget that increased taxes, but the veto was overridden.

The two chambers of Congress are responsible for enacting laws at the federal level.

Law at the Federal Level

At the federal level, lawmaking is much the same as at the state level, except different people are involved. Just as the state government is divided into two chambers, so is the federal government. At the federal level, the two chambers of the legislative branch of government are the Senate and the House of Representatives.

Each state has two senators in the United States Senate, so the total number of senators is 100. The total number of members of the House of Representatives is 435. This total is based on state populations. The states with greater populations have more representatives than the states with lesser populations. Even the smallest and least-populated states have three representatives—that is the minimum number per state. California has 55, which is the greatest number of representatives in the House.

Just as in state government, federal laws originate in either the House or the Senate. The idea for new legislation can come from anyone—from the president of the United States to a U.S. citizen—but a member of Congress must propose the actual legislation.

Once legislation is proposed, it goes through a similar process to the state process. It is assigned to a committee or subcommittee, then reviewed, researched, debated, and amended in the chamber in which it was introduced. Eventually, it comes to the chamber floor for a vote.

If it passes that vote, similar legislation is introduced in the other chamber of Congress. The process is much the same: It is assigned to a committee or subcommittee, and it is researched, reviewed, debated, and amended. Eventually, the proposed legislation comes to the floor for a vote.

If the vote passes in both chambers, the two bills are compared. One final bill is compiled and, it is hoped, approved by both chambers of Congress. At that point, it goes to the president of the United States for his signature. Once signed, the bill becomes federal law.

If the president chooses not to sign the bill, the options are similar to those at the state level: they can veto the bill, or they can simply ignore it and let it be a pocket veto. And similar to the state level, the chambers of Congress have the power to override presidential vetoes with a two-thirds vote in both chambers.

The Supreme Law of the Land

At the very top of the system is the Constitution. If an issue cannot be settled by following local, state, or federal law and precedent, it eventually becomes a matter settled by constitutional law. Marriage equality is a good example. For a very long time, marriage in the United States was defined as being between a man and a woman. However, same-sex couples began to argue that it was unconstitutional (against the Constitution) to enforce this, because the Constitution itself does not define what marriage is.

State laws were in place to enforce the fact that legal marriages could exist only between a man and a woman. Eventually, some states began to change their laws to allow for marriage between same-sex couples. This still left these couples without certain federal rights, so they took their argument to the federal courts.

The argument eventually made it all the way to the Supreme Court where the landmark case of *Obergefell v. Hodges* was decided in 2015. The Supreme Court ruled that even though marriage is not mentioned in the Constitution, the Fourteenth Amendment—specifically, the Due Process and Equal Protection clauses—grants same-sex couples the same rights as heterosexual couples. The *Obergefell v. Hodges* ruling required all states to recognize same-sex marriages.

Other major issues have come to the Supreme Court when they could not be decided in lower courts and by state and local law. These include abortion rights, affirmative action, education rights, disability rights, and civil rights cases.

In 2015, *Obergefell v. Hodges* changed the face of marriage law in the United States when the Supreme Court ruled in favor of marriage equality.

CHAPTER 3

Crime and Punishment

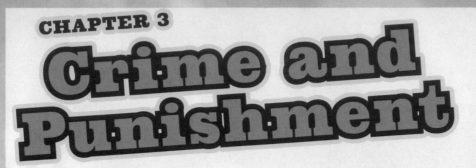

How crimes are punished depends on the type of crime and the law that was violated. The double-jeopardy clause in the Fifth Amendment does not allow a person to be charged twice for the same crime. Crimes are classified as infractions, misdemeanors, and felonies. How a crime is charged will determine the punishment.

Infractions

IT'S THE LAW

clean up after your dog | **DON'T LITTER**

MAXIMUM FINE $450

Usually, breaking a local ordinance is an infraction and does not result in an arrest.

Infractions, or petty offenses, are violations of local ordinances, **municipal codes**, administrative regulations, and sometimes minor traffic rules. Many states do not consider infractions to be criminal offenses, so they are not punishable by jail time. Instead, a fine may be attached to the infraction.

Citizens can argue infractions. If a person is issued a citation (a fine) for an infraction, they can pay it or they can go to court and present their case to the judge. Infractions do not give the person an automatic right to a jury trial and free legal counsel as more serious crimes do. But they do give a person the right to be heard before a judge. Many people choose to go to traffic court to argue traffic tickets, though many others simply choose to pay the fine.

Perpetrators can be arrested for misdemeanors, although jail time for these crimes is usually minimal.

Misdemeanors

Misdemeanors are more serious than infractions, but less serious than felonies. Punishment for misdemeanors often involves a fine and time in a county jail. Misdemeanors cover a broad range of crimes, so they are often separated into three different types: petty, ordinary, and high or gross.

Usually for a petty misdemeanor conviction, the person faces a relatively small fine and a jail sentence of fewer than six months. Ordinary and high or gross misdemeanors carry more jail time and bigger fines. However, the jail time is usually served at a county jail rather than at a state or federal prison.

While infractions are typically charged at the local level (though there are some federal infractions), misdemeanors are punishable at the state or federal level. At the state level, lawyers and judges typically have a little flexibility in exactly how to charge the crime and sentence the **defendant** for it. However, there is very little flexibility in misdemeanors charged under federal law. For those, judges follow strict federal guidelines for sentencing. These guidelines take into account the severity of the crime, the defendant's criminal history, and other factors.

Federal misdemeanors fall into classes A, B, and C for punishment and sentencing. Federal Class A misdemeanors can yield six months to a year in jail for the defendant. Federal Class B misdemeanors can result in anywhere from 30 days to 6 months in jail. Federal Class C misdemeanors result in 5 to 30 days in jail.

HOW WELL DO YOU UNDERSTAND AMERICAN DEMOCRACY?

The National Institute of Justice has stated that prison is not an effective deterrent for crime, and harsher punishments are no more effective at deterring crime than lesser punishments. What are some alternatives to harsh prison sentences that you think might be effective in deterring crime and lowering the number of repeat offenders?

Felonies

Felonies are the most serious crimes under the law of the United States. They include crimes such as murder, arson, kidnapping, burglary, and terrorism, among others. Like misdemeanors, felonies are sometimes separated into different classes, with more serious crimes receiving harsher punishments. Repeat offenders also receive harsher punishments than first-time offenders. Felonies are usually punishable by a sizable fine or a prison sentence of more than a year—or both. The punishment will vary, depending on the crime and the defendant's history.

Many states have three-strikes laws for felonies. This means that when a person is convicted of their third felony offense, their punishment is quite severe—often life in prison. If the person's two previous offenses were for serious crimes, such as arson and kidnapping, they would be subject to life in prison for a third offense. This applies even if that offense were for something as minor as stealing a loaf of bread. Opponents of three-strikes laws argue that, in theory, a person could be sentenced to life in prison for a relatively minor offense.

But every state that has a three-strikes law also has a provision that goes with it. This provision allows a judge to sentence a defendant to probation for the third crime, if the third crime is trivial in nature.

TRIBAL LAW

A unique situation occurs in the case of Native American reservation lands. Native Americans living on federal Indian reservations live according to federal and tribal laws. Native American tribes have sovereignty, so the tribes living on reservations are self-governing. However, just as states are sovereign and yet still a part of the United States, so are reservations. So, Native Americans live under tribal law but also under federal law.

This is why casinos and gambling facilities can exist on reservations. Most states have laws prohibiting gambling (Nevada and New Jersey being notable exceptions). However, tribal law takes precedence over state law on a reservation. So, in a state such as Arizona, where gambling is generally illegal, casinos and gambling facilities can exist on the reservation. And non-Native citizens are free to enter the reservation and gamble at the casinos.

Native lands operate under tribal law in addition to federal law. The tribal laws may differ from state laws, though often they are fairly similar.

ENTERING PINE RIDGE INDIAN RESERVATION

CHAPTER 4

Types of Courts

There are numerous types of courts in the United States. At their most basic level, they are divided into federal courts and state courts. The cases heard in each type of court depend on the type of case (civil or criminal), as well as the law that was violated (for example, state law or federal law).

Criminal Cases and Civil Cases

To understand how cases are heard in the court system, it is important to recognize the difference between criminal cases and civil cases. Criminal cases are those in which an action that is harmful to a person or to society as a whole has been committed. Examples include murder, arson, terrorism, and rape cases, as well as lesser crimes such as burglary. In all of those types of case, one or more people have been harmed in some way—either by loss of property or by personal injury or death.

The Boston Marathon bombing in 2013 was a criminal case in which multiple lives were endangered.

Civil cases are usually disputes between people or organizations in which one party (the **plaintiff**) seeks to receive compensation from another party (the defendant). The compensation may be monetary, but it could also involve the defendant fulfilling the terms of some agreement that they did not previously fulfill.

Criminal and civil cases can be heard in either state or federal courts. Where they are heard depends on the terms of the case and the parties involved. A civil suit might be heard in state court if it involves two parties who had a contract, and the defendant did not fulfill the terms of the contract. If the civil case involves one party violating federal statutes (laws) or the Constitution, then it will be heard in federal court. An example of this might be a person suing a police department that denied them the right to assemble peacefully at a protest rally.

Identity theft and certain cybercrimes are heard at the federal level.

Criminal cases heard in state court involve issues that are not a violation of federal law or the Constitution. For example, murder is a violation of federal law, but it is also a violation of state laws. So, a murder case is typically heard in a state court—no need to take it to the federal level. However, there are a number of crimes that are heard at the federal level, such as identity theft, aircraft hijacking, tax evasion, counterfeiting, and assassinating the president or vice president. Any of those cases, and a number of others, proceed straight to federal court.

DOUBLE JEOPARDY—OR NOT?

Although the double jeopardy clause of the Fifth Amendment protects people from being charged with the same crime twice, there is a way around this. A person can be charged in both a criminal and a civil suit for the same crime. One well-known example is the trial of football legend O.J. Simpson, which took place in the mid-1990s. Simpson was accused of killing his estranged wife, Nicole Brown Simpson, and Ronald Goldman.

The televised criminal trial caught the interest of millions of Americans. People were glued to their televisions as they waited to see whether the prosecution could prove beyond a reasonable doubt that Simpson killed the two. In the end, Simpson was found not guilty, much to the anguish of the victims' families. However, Simpson was also charged in a wrongful death civil suit for the same two deaths. He was found guilty in that case and ordered to pay the families $25 million.

He was found not guilty in the criminal case, but guilty in the civil case, because the required level of proof is less in a civil case. Jurors believed Simpson killed Brown and Goldman, and they found him guilty of the civil suit. But there was a shred of doubt that made it impossible for a separate jury to convict him in the criminal suit.

The world reeled when Simpson was found not guilty of criminal homicide. He was later found guilty in a civil suit.

The Federal Court System

The federal court system is divided into three basic levels: district courts, circuit courts, and the Supreme Court. Each level has a distinct purpose.

District Courts

The lowest courts in the federal court hierarchy are the district courts. These are also referred to as trial courts. Throughout the United States, there are 94 district courts. Each district court is overseen by at least one district judge, who is appointed by the president of the United States and confirmed by the Senate. District judges serve for life, though they can be **impeached** by Congress if their ability to do their job ethically comes into question. Currently, there are more than 670 district judges in the United States.

For civil cases, any case regarding a violation of federal statute, **treaties**, or the Constitution, is first heard in federal district court. If the case also violates state law, then the plaintiff can decide whether to bring the case to federal or state court. There are some cases that are entirely based on state law, but can still be heard in federal court. But there are strict rules about this. For example, the financial amount must be greater than $75,000, and the defendants and plaintiffs must be in different states. This unique situation is called diversity jurisdiction, and it applies only to civil cases.

District courts are the lowest courts in the federal court system. This is the federal courthouse at Beaumont, Texas.

For criminal cases, there is no such thing as diversity jurisdiction. Criminal cases that violate state law are heard in state courts, and cases that violate federal law are heard in federal court. Some criminal acts violate both state and federal laws. For example, murder is always illegal—at the state level and the federal level. However, murder would usually be tried at the state level first. If the prosecution does not get a conviction at the state level, it could choose to pursue a case in federal court. The double-jeopardy clause does not apply when it comes to cases that violate both state and federal laws. However, not all prosecutors will attempt this. They determine whether the likelihood of getting a conviction in federal court is worth the time, effort, and money they would have to spend getting the case heard in federal court.

Circuit Courts

If a case is heard in federal district court, and one party is unhappy with the outcome, it can appeal to a circuit court. This is also called a court of appeals. In the United States, there are 12 federal circuits. Each circuit has a court, and each circuit court has multiple judges who preside over it. These judges are appointed by the president and confirmed by the Senate, just like district judges. Circuit court judges also have a lifetime appointment and can be impeached. The number of judges per circuit court ranges from 6 to 29.

When a case from district court is brought to a circuit court, the case is first heard by a panel of three circuit court judges. Parties representing the defendant and the plaintiff submit briefs (written arguments). Briefs detail why the party feels the district court's decision should be upheld or reversed. Once the briefs are filed, the circuit court schedules oral arguments. This allows legal representatives for both parties to make their arguments and answer any questions the judges may have.

The Supreme Court

If a party is still unhappy with the decision of the district court, then the case can be brought to the Supreme Court. The Supreme Court is made up of nine justices—eight associate justices and one chief justice. Like the judges in the lower federal courts, these justices are appointed by the president and confirmed by the Senate, and their appointments are lifelong.

The process of appeal to the Supreme Court is a bit different from in the circuit courts. The circuit court must hear an appeal to any case brought up from a district court. However, the Supreme Court has the right to refuse to hear a case brought from circuit court.

The parties involved can file a **writ of certiorari**, which asks the Supreme Court to hear the case. The court will then decide whether to grant it. If they do grant it, the parties involved file briefs and make oral arguments in front of the Supreme Court. The Supreme Court typically grants these hearings in fewer than 1 percent of cases brought up from the circuit court. If the Supreme Court declines to hear an appeal, then the decision made in the circuit court stands.

In front of the Supreme Court sits a statue of Chief Justice John Marshall. He was the fourth Chief Justice of the Supreme Court and served as Chief Justice from 1801 to 1835.

The Supreme Court can also hear cases brought up from the highest state courts. One good example is *Endrew F. v. Douglas County School District*. This case began in Colorado state courts, but it eventually made its way to to the Supreme Court. The plaintiff's legal team had successfully argued that the case was about a violation of federal law (the Individuals with Disabilities Education Act, or IDEA). The case began as a suit between the family of a student with a disability and the school district in question. But it became an issue of civil rights when the plaintiffs successfully argued that federal law was being violated. It was then heard by the Supreme Court.

HOW WELL DO YOU UNDERSTAND AMERICAN DEMOCRACY?

The Supreme Court has made numerous landmark decisions that have changed the face of U.S. society in terms of women's rights, marriage equality, civil rights, education, and more. What major issues can you think of that might be affected by Supreme Court rulings in the coming years?

The Supreme Court typically has nine justices sitting on it at any given time. In the center of the first row is Edward Douglass White Jr., who was the ninth Chief Justice of the United States. He served on the Supreme Court from 1894 to 1921.

State Courts

The federal court system is fairly straightforward: there are district courts, then circuit courts, and finally the Supreme Court. However, the state court system is not necessarily as clearly defined. It depends on the state, because each state has its own system. Most states, though, follow a fairly similar structure to the federal court system.

In most states, the lowest level of courts are trial courts, which are often superior courts. However, there are special trial courts that are not superior courts. This is where most cases are heard at the state level, though there are certain specialty courts for specific types of cases, too.

If a party involved in a case is unhappy with the decision made in trial court, the party may take it to the next level. This is generally the intermediate appellate court, or intermediate court of appeals. In this type of court, the judge just considers how the law was applied in the original ruling. They do not typically hear the facts of the case again. The case is not being retried in appellate court. The party who is unhappy with the lower court's decision is simply arguing why it believes the laws were not applied fairly in the ruling.

If a party is still unhappy with a decision at the appellate level, then the case can be taken to the state Supreme Court. Like the intermediate appellate court, the state Supreme Court typically just hears arguments on why state law may have been improperly applied in the original decision. It does not hear the entire case being retried.

This is usually how the state court systems work, though specifics may differ from state to state. For example, divorce cases in some states are heard in family court, while in other states, they are heard in superior court. Some states may have separate courts designated for civil and criminal cases. Other states may hear both types of cases in the same court.

CHAPTER 5

Specific Subject Courts

At the federal and the state levels, there are special courts designated to handle specific cases.

Special State Courts

At the state level, many cases are first heard in superior courts, which are general jurisdiction trial courts. However, some cases are heard at courts with special or limited jurisdiction. The structure differs from state to state. For example, in some states, small claims court is a separate entity from trial courts. In other states, small claims are handled in a particular division of the trial court.

Probate Courts

Probate courts handle matters dealing with estates and wills. When a person dies and there is a dispute over their assets, the matter is generally heard in probate court. In some states, probate courts also oversee guardianships, adoptions, and **competency hearings**.

Family Courts and Juvenile Courts

Family courts hear cases related to custody disputes, child support, neglect and abuse, and sometimes juvenile crime. In states where juvenile crimes are not heard in family courts, they are often heard in juvenile courts. Usually, juvenile crimes include those committed by individuals who are younger than either 16 or 18, depending on the state.

If an individual is older than that maximum age, the superior court may determine whether the person should be tried as an adult.

Traffic Courts

Traffic courts involve traffic violations. If a person receives a ticket they think is unfair, they can go to traffic court to dispute it, or they can simply pay the fine. Traffic courts usually do not handle cases involving traffic accidents. Those are handled between the parties involved in the appropriate court for the dispute. For example, often these are civil cases and so are heard in the appropriate civil court.

HOW WELL DO YOU UNDERSTAND AMERICAN DEMOCRACY?

When a teenager approaching adulthood commits a serious crime, there is often the question of whether the teen should be charged as an adult. Under what circumstances do you think it is appropriate for a teenager to be charged as an adult? What guidelines would you create to use in this situation?

Many states have separate traffic courts that are specifically for traffic-related violations.

33

Small Claims Courts

Small claims courts are for civil suits in which the dollar amount is below a certain limit. The limit varies by state, but is usually between $3,000 and $7,500. People often use small claims courts for issues such as a contractor not completing work in a satisfactory manner. A contractor might take a customer to small claims court if they have refused to pay after work was completed.

Housing Courts

Housing courts hear disputes between tenants and landlords. For example, if a landlord wishes to evict a tenant and the tenant refuses to leave the property, the landlord may take the matter to housing court. If it is a matter of money—for example, when a landlord refuses to return a deposit to a tenant when the tenant moves out—the case may be handled in housing court. It may also be handled in small claims courts, depending on how the state's special court system is structured.

Disputes between tenants and landlords are not uncommon in rental markets, and they are often handled in special housing courts.

Special Federal Courts

At the federal level, special courts include the U.S. Court of Federal Claims, the U.S. Tax Court, the U.S. Court of Appeals for Veterans Claims, the U.S. Court of International Trade, and **admiralty** courts.

Court of Federal Claims

If a person or party has a claim against the federal government that is based on the Constitution, federal statute, or federal regulations, it is heard in the U.S. Court of Federal Claims.

Tax Court

The U.S. Tax Court is where individuals dispute tax-related issues. For example, if the Internal Revenue Service (IRS) tells a taxpayer that they owe more taxes than they think they owe, that taxpayer has the right to dispute the amount in the U.S. Tax Court.

Court of Appeals for Veterans Claims

If a veteran or their dependents has requested benefits from the Department of Veteran Affairs and been denied, that individual can take up the matter in the Court of Appeals for Veterans Claims.

Court of International Trade

The U.S. Court of International Trade hears civil cases that arise in relation to international trade and import transactions.

Admiralty Courts

Admiralty courts hear cases involving admiralty and **maritime** actions, including **torts**, injuries, and maritime contracts.

SPECIAL COURTS OF THE PAST

Some special federal courts were created, then eventually disbanded when they were no longer needed. One example is the United States Court for China, which existed from 1906 to 1943. This court was in China and was created to hear the cases of U.S. citizens arrested in China.

The court heard civil and criminal cases, but the cases had to meet certain criteria, such as the potential punishment not exceeding a maximum fine or length of imprisonment. The court was abolished in 1943 by a mutual treaty between the United States and China. This resulted from the United States declaring war on Japan.

Another special court that existed for a limited time was the United States Court for Berlin. This court existed from 1955 to 1990, during part of the Cold War years. It was created to hear cases in the section of Berlin that Americans occupied.

However, the United States Court for Berlin heard only one case, in 1979. It convened to hear the case of East German hijackers of LOT Polish Airlines Flight 165. The hijackers boarded the East Germany–bound plane in Poland, in an attempt to have it land in West Germany. They planned to seek political asylum there. At that time, East Germany was a communist country, and its citizens lived under oppression. The hijackers succeeded in getting the plane to land (safely) in West Germany. However, they faced charges for hijacking the plane. Their case was heard in the United States Court for Berlin, since East Germany had recently signed a hijacking treaty.

The armed forces have special courts for their members. Officers are tried there for things such as insubordination, as was the case here in 1925 at the **court-martial** of Colonel Billy Mitchell.

Military Courts

When a member of the armed forces faces legal judgment, it is handled in military court. There are different types of military courts, including the U.S. Court of Appeals for the Armed Forces, and courts of military review or court-martial.

Bankruptcy Courts

Bankruptcy proceedings are handled through federal bankruptcy courts. There are numerous types of bankruptcies, for individuals and for companies. All are handled in federal bankruptcy courts.

Courts for the Trial of Impeachments

These courts are specifically designed for impeachment hearings. The best-known court is probably the Senate, which acts as the Court for the Trial of Impeachments when proceedings are brought against a president or vice president.

The Supreme Court

The Supreme Court is the highest court in the United States. When cases have worked their way through the lower courts, and the parties are not satisfied with the judgments, they may come before the Supreme Court. However, this is a very big "may." The Supreme Court has the right to refuse to hear cases, and it often does.

Typically, the Supreme Court will hear cases where it is possible that constitutional law has been violated, or where the outcome may significantly affect U.S. law and policy. The Supreme Court will not, for example, hear a case in which one party of a divorcing couple is unhappy with the settlement judgment. Such a case has bearing only on the couple and their immediate family. However, the Supreme Court did hear a case on marriage that led them to rule that the federal government and all states must recognize same-sex marriages. So it is not so much the subject matter that determines whether the Supreme Court will hear a case. It is whether the case will have an impact on U.S. law and policy.

Impact of Supreme Court Rulings

When the Supreme Court rules on a case, the impact can be enormous. In the U.S. legal system, lawyers and judges rely on several things when arguing and deciding cases. One factor is laws and ordinances at the local, state, federal, and constitutional levels. If a defendant has clearly violated a law, the case is straightforward.

When the Supreme Court ruled in favor of marriage equality in 2015, an enormous crowd gathered outside to celebrate the victory.

However, with laws there are gray areas. This is true even for very serious crimes, such as murder. Murder is illegal—but killing someone in self-defense is not. If the defendant claims they acted in self-defense, then their lawyers will work to prove that in court so the defendant will not be found guilty of murder.

There are also different types of crimes. For example, first-degree murder with special circumstances (such as premeditation and lying in wait for the victim) can be punishable by the death penalty in some states. Then there are also cases of **justifiable homicide**, **manslaughter**, **second-degree murder**, **vehicular homicide**, and the like, making things a lot more complicated.

The fact that there are different types of crimes means that prosecution, conviction, and punishment are not really so simple. As a result, lawyers and judges turn to another factor: legal precedent. Most cases that come before the court have similarities to past cases, and lawyers will look to the rulings in these past cases. If it helps their case, they will present the past judgment to the judge as a reason why their client should receive a similar judgment.

One good example is the landmark 1954 Supreme Court decision in *Brown v. Board of Education*. That case involved racial segregation in schools. An 1896 Supreme Court case, *Plessy v. Ferguson*, established that black students and white students can be educated in separate schools as long as the facilities are equal. However, the reality was that the facilities were often not equal. Schools for black students were often underfunded, understaffed, and/or staffed with unprepared teachers. Schools for white students generally had better funding and more qualified staff.

Brown v. Board of Education sought to overturn *Plessy v. Ferguson*, and the case made it to the Supreme Court. *Plessy v. Ferguson* was the legal precedent under which lawyers had been arguing similar educational segregation cases and judges had been ruling on them. But the Supreme Court eventually ruled in favor of the plaintiffs in *Brown v. Board of Education*, which led to the eventual desegregation of schools. This also overturned the *Plessy v. Ferguson* decision. From that point forward, *Brown v. Board of Education* was established as legal precedent.

If *Brown v. Board of Education* had been about just one child in one school, it never would have made it to the Supreme Court. However, it was an issue that affected black students everywhere. Even in the initial lawsuit (filed in Kansas), there was more than one plaintiff. Oliver Brown was just one of many frustrated parents. His child was forced to be bussed to a black school rather than attending her neighborhood school just a few blocks from their house, solely because she was black. The Supreme Court recognized that the initial lawsuit was symbolic of a much bigger problem, so it heard the case. If it had not heard the case, segregated schools might still exist. The impact of landmark Supreme Court decisions such as *Brown v. Board of Education* cannot be overstated. They have the potential to change how U.S. society functions.

Landmark Supreme Court Rulings

The Supreme Court has heard and decided on many important cases. But a few stand out as landmarks that changed the fundamental belief structure in the United States. *Brown v. Board of Education* is one, as is *Obergefell v. Hodges* (the 2015 ruling that granted same-sex couples the right to have their marriage recognized in all states). There are many others, too.

Roe v. Wade

In 1973, the Supreme Court ruled on *Roe v. Wade*, which may be one of the best-known landmark cases. In the simplest terms, this ruling made abortion legal in the United States. However, there were certain limitations attached, such as the fact that states could regulate how far into a pregnancy an abortion could be performed.

HOW WELL DO YOU UNDERSTAND AMERICAN DEMOCRACY?

With a little research, you can learn about other landmark Supreme Court decisions. Are there any that you disagree with? *Roe v. Wade* has long been a controversial decision, as is *Obergefell v. Hodges*. What about you? What landmark decisions do you agree or disagree with, and why?

More than 40 years after the Supreme Court ruling, there are still people who want the court to overturn *Roe v. Wade*.

Dred Scott v. Sandford

Often known as the Dred Scott case, this 1857 Supreme Court decision ruled that black people—whether free or enslaved—were not U.S. citizens and so could not sue in federal court for their freedom. Dred Scott was a slave who had been taken to free states during his enslavement. When his master died, he attempted to sue for his freedom. His suit was denied because, according to the Supreme Court, he did not meet the criteria of a U.S. citizen. It was a huge blow for slaves' rights.

The Supreme Court ruled that Dred Scott was not a citizen. This demonstrates the potential danger of Supreme Court rulings.

Regents of the U. of California v. Bakke

This 1978 case changed the face of affirmative action. Affirmative action was established to try to level the playing field for minority citizens with respect to higher education and employment. Universities often used racial quotas to comply with affirmative action guidelines. For example, they would admit a certain percentage of black students each year. A white student, Allan Bakke, was denied entry to medical school at the University of California at Davis. However, minority students with lower grade point averages and test scores were admitted. Bakke argued that the racial quotas that gave minority students admission over him were a violation of the equal protection clause in the Constitution. The Supreme Court ruled in Bakke's favor and against the strict use of racial quotas in college admissions. However, the Supreme Court did establish that race is admissible as an admissions criterion.

A Complex System

The U.S. legal and judicial system is both complex and simple. It is made up of many pieces and branches, which have put forth numerous laws and ordinances. Over all this lie the words of the Constitution and the decisions of the Supreme Court. It is all part of an intricate puzzle. Crimes are tried and punishments decided in the appropriate courts based on the applicable laws. With this comes a dash of flair from lawyers whose job is to find legal precedent to achieve the best possible ruling for their client.

Does this complex system work? That is hard to say, and it depends on who you ask. Some think it works very well, some think sentences are too harsh or biased, and some think crime rates could be lower. There are parts of the United States where crime rates are very high and citizens long for a good solution. But what is the solution? More laws and more regulations? Or fewer laws and more self-government? That, too, depends on who you ask.

It is up to individual citizens to understand the laws in place in the United States, and how to live under them. And if they do not choose to live by those laws, smart citizens will understand how the judicial system works and what their rights in it are.

Affirmative action was put in place to level the playing field for minorities in academia.

VISUAL SUMMARY

The U.S. Judicial System in Action

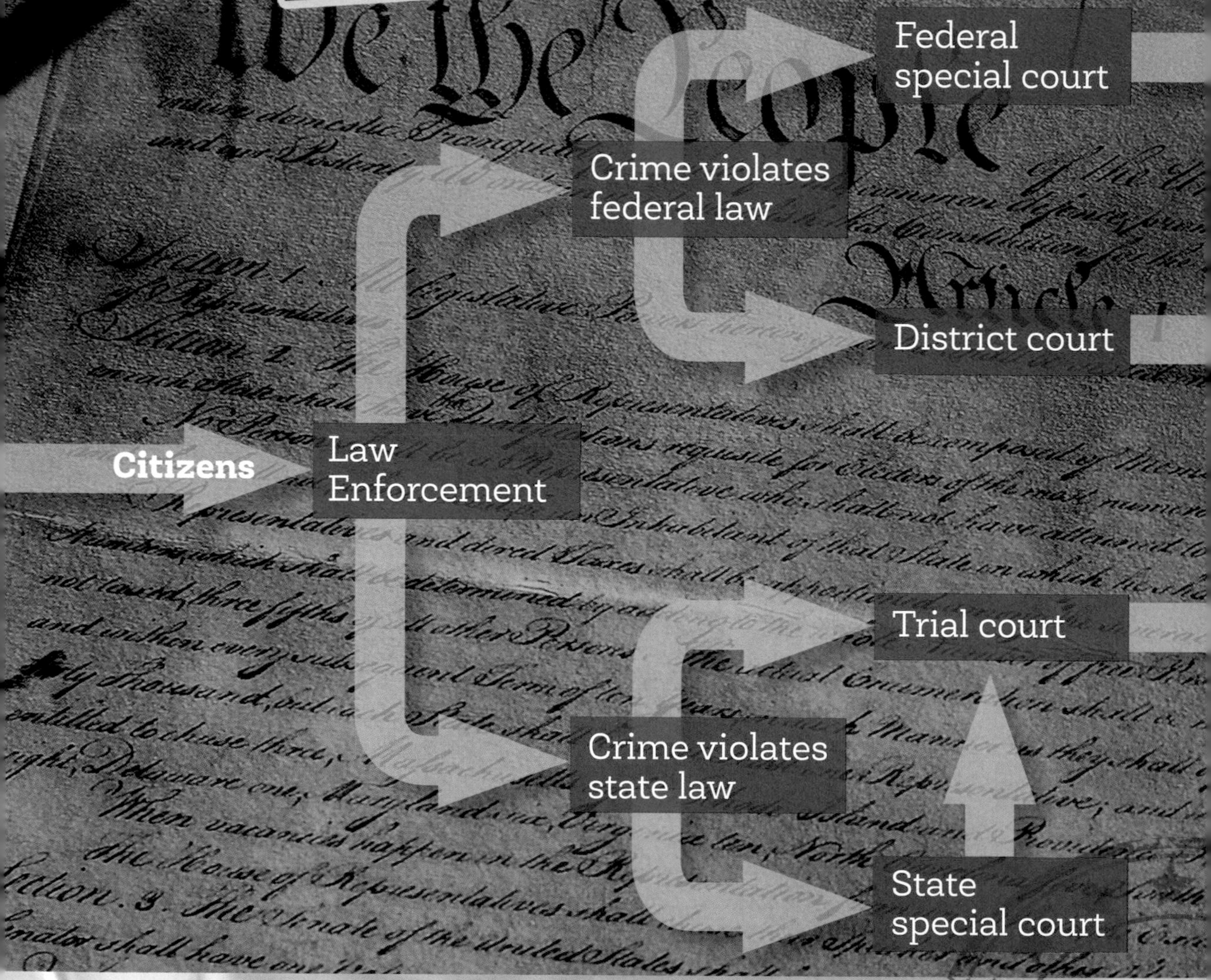
Citizens
Law Enforcement
Crime violates federal law
Federal special court
District court
Crime violates state law
Trial court
State special court

This diagram shows the U.S. court system: If a citizen violates a federal law, the case passes to a district court or a federal special court. The case may then also go to appeal, and then all the way to the Supreme Court. If a citizen violates a state law, the case goes to a trial court or a state special court. The case may then go to appeal, and then all the way to the Supreme Court.

Designated court of appeals

Circuit court

Appellate

United States Supreme Court

State Supreme Court

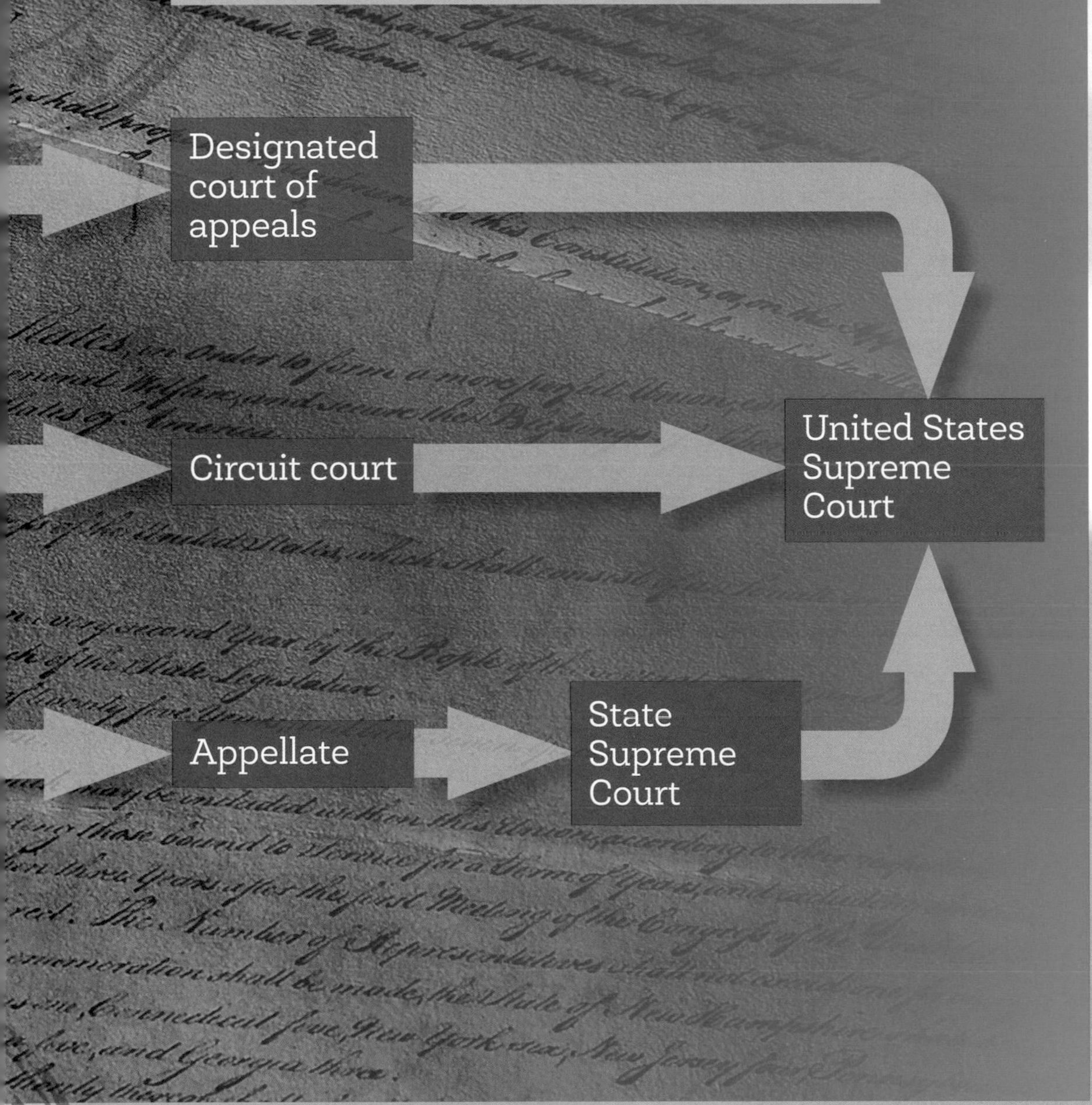

Glossary

admiralty Jurisdiction of courts over cases related to ships, the sea, or other waters.

civil rights The rights of all citizens to political and social freedom, and to equality.

codified Formally arranged into a systematic collection of laws.

Cold War The period roughly from 1947 to 1991 in which the United States and the Soviet Union were engaged in a delicate balance of power with the goal of preventing nuclear war from breaking out.

competency hearings Hearings designed to determine whether a defendant in a court case is mentally competent to stand trial.

conservative Describes one who values traditional systems and is cautious about new innovation.

court-martial A hearing in a special court for a member of the armed services who is accused of an offense against military law.

defendant A person or party accused in a court of law.

dictatorship A country ruled by a person who has total power that was usually gained by force.

Framers of the Constitution The delegates who went to the Constitutional Convention and drafted the Constitution.

impeached Charged of misconduct against a holder of public office.

justifiable homicide Killing that is found to be without criminal intent, such as killing a person in self-defense or in defense of another person.

manslaughter Killing a person without planning ahead to do so.

maritime Related to the sea.

municipal codes Laws put forth and enforced by a specific municipality.

municipality A city or town with corporate status and a local government.

oligarchy A country ruled by a small group of people.

plaintiff A person who brings a case against a defendant in court.

precedence Priority in importance.

second-degree murder Murder that was not planned beforehand but that does indicate malice aforethought.

sovereign Acting independently, without outside interference.

subdivision A planned housing area.

torts Wrongful acts that lead to civil legal liability.

treaties Formal, ratified agreements between two or more countries.

vehicular homicide A crime involving the death of a person other than the driver if the driver was found to either be criminally negligent or have operated a motor vehicle in a murderous manner, such as purposely running someone over.

veto To reject a proposed law.

writ of certiorari An order for a lower court to deliver its ruling to a higher court so that it may be reviewed.

For More Information

Books

Fremon, David K. *The Jim Crow Laws and Racism in United States History*. New York, NY: Enslow Publishing, 2014.

Furi-Perry, Ursula. *Going to Court: An Introduction to the U.S. Justice System*. Chicago, IL: American Bar Association, 2015.

Herda, D.J. *Slavery and Citizenship: The Dred Scott Case*. New York, NY: Enslow Publishing, 2017.

Madani, Hamed. *The Supreme Court and the Judicial Branch: How the Federal Courts Interpret Our Laws*. New York, NY: Enslow Publishing, 2012.

Websites

The FindLaw website allows users to search for information about various legal and judicial topics. It also presents simple explanations for a vast number of topics:
www.findlaw.com

This site has links to pages with detailed information about landmark Supreme Court decisions:
landmarkcases.org/en/landmark/home

This site provides easy-to-understand explanations for many landmark cases heard in the Supreme Court:
www.uscourts.gov/about-federal-courts/educational-resources/supreme-court-landmarks

The White House website has a page devoted to the judicial branch that covers the basics of how that branch of government works:
www.whitehouse.gov/1600/judicial-branch